D1621182

# GIN
# SNOB'S
## GUIDE

BB

www.booksbyboxer.com

Published in the UK by
Books By Boxer, Leeds, LS13 4BS
© Books By Boxer 2018
All Rights Reserved

ISBN: 9781909732605

time to drink gin

# GIN-TERPRETATION

**snob** | sno-b |

*noun*

1. A person with an exaggerated respect for high social position or wealth who seeks to associate with social superiors and looks down on those regarded as socially inferior.

Example sentence: 'Her mother was a snob and would keep no beer in the house, only gin'.

1.1 with adjective or noun modifier.
A person who believes that their tastes in a particular area are superior to those of other people.
'A gin snob.'

# gin | gi-n |

*noun*

1. A clear alcoholic spirit distilled from grain or malt and flavoured with juniper berries.

*origin*

The word 'Gin' is an abbreviation of 'Genever' the original Dutch alcoholic drink from whence 'gin' is derived.

**gin snob** | gi-n • sno-b |

*noun*

A person with an exaggerated respect for Gin who considers others, on the subject of Gin, to be socially inferior (or who thinks their knowledge of Gin is more superior than most others).

# GIN

This guide is designed to aid Gin snobbery, Gin knowledge, Gin drinking and all the essential paraphernalia that is associated with this important pastime.

It is intended to improve and augment your mastery of the facts and to provide the essentials necessary to enhance your appreciation of the silver nectar, the tipple of the Gods, that is especially refreshing in the garden as the evening sun of a summer's day gently descends towards the horizon.

It is not purely about taste. It is about knowledge, acquired, cultivated wisdom, honed and refined by a cultured mind, and the application of this knowledge in choosing all the right constituents to create an ethereal experience in which to appreciate the pleasure of a true Gin and Tonic.

# *The* AGE *Of* GINNOCENCE

If you were to visit most pubs and bars in the UK 10 or 15 years ago and ask for a 'Gin and Tonic', you would get precisely that. The gin was usually a gin of the type that the bar owner got a good deal on, a 'Gordon's' or a 'Beefeater' and the tonic was invariably 'Schweppes'. How the world has changed. There are literally thousands of different gin brands, from those who only produce a few bottles a year to the massive international distilleries whose output is millions of litres.

Perhaps what has led the 'Gin Revolution' (or as a result of it) is the plethora of hundreds of different types of tonic water and other interesting mixers to add to your favourite tipple. Whether you just need a splash of tonic or the more usual mix which is 2 parts mixer to 1 part gin. Fever Tree and Fentiman's, to name but 2 among many quality tonic brands, can hold legitimate claim to the higher end of the tonic market.

However, at the other end of the spectrum, a decent gin can be abased by a squirt from a hose-type, soft drinks dispenser.

# GINNOVATION

In the years since 2010 the number of gin makers has more than trebled.

It would seem that anyone with only a vague knowledge of how to turn flavourless grain alcohol into an acceptable aperitif by the addition of juniper berries and a selection of fruits and spices can now become a gin distiller and some of these newer brands are distillations of distinction.

# *In* WITH *The* GIN CROWD

From being the poor relation to a whisky or a Cognac, gin has now become the number one spirit of choice for discerning connoisseurs of fine, distilled alcohol.

Gin satisfies those merely requiring a refresher or a reviver and offers a range of choice for the 'Gin Snob' who will only drink the rarest and most expensive brands.

For the modest imbiber or party animals on the road to temporary self-destruction… gin is in!

# GINEBRIATION

As with vodka and other clear spirits there is a misconception that you will escape without suffering a thumping hangover in the morning after a night of Gindulgence... drinking too much gin.

A gin or vodka hangover is less severe than a whisky, rum or brandy one, as these contain characteristics other than pure spirit.

The juniper berry, an integral ingredient of gin, is a diuretic (makes you pee more) and so increases the dehydration affect of alcohol, a key factor of hangover severity.

GIN LANE.

Gin cursed Fiend, with Fury fraught,
Makes human Race a Prey.
It enters by a deadly Draught
And steals our Life away.

Virtue and Truth, driv'n to Despair,
Its Rage compells to fly,
But cherishes with hellish Care
Theft, Murder, Perjury.

Damn'd Cup! that on the Vitals preys,
That liquid Fire contains,
Which Madness to the Heart conveys,
And rolls it thro' the Veins.

# GIN
## *Olden* TIMES

'Drunk for a penny, dead drunk for two pence'. These words are etched on the side of, 'The Gin Royal' (a 'gin house') that was immortalised in 'Gin Lane', one of the most famous and iconic engravings by Hogarth in 1750. It's a damning imputation on the evils of gin.

Amongst other sobering depictions in this picture there is in the foreground a woman lolling on the steps in drunken disarray, her baby falling to its death at the side of her. Hogarth's prints were intended to show the wickedness of the 'gin trade' that created such an epidemic, starting in the late 1600's and carrying on for many years.

# GINSANE

Gin, cursed fiend with fury fraught,
Makes human race a prey,
It enters by a deadly draught,
And steals our life away.
Virtue and truth driv'n to despair,
It's rage compels to fly,
But cherishes with hellish care,
Theft, murder, perjury
Damn cup that on the vitals preys,
That liquid fire contains,
Which madness to the heart conveys,
and rolls it through the veins.

A poem that accompanied the publication
of Hogarth's print, 'Gin Lane', 1750.

# SIN GIN

It was the crack cocaine or crystal meth of it's day carrying along with it prostitution, robbery and violent crime. Over a quarter of all premises in the parish of St. Giles, London, were gin houses.

The 'Gin Act' of 1736 that required distillers to pay a whopping (at the time) £50 annual license, barely stopped the flow. The trade went underground and the quality of the product lowered to dangerous levels with the use of wood alcohol, turpentine and other poisons.

# BEER **GOOD**, GIN **BAD**

Hogarth was not against alcohol usage. His other engraving produced at the same time as 'Gin Lane' was 'Beer Street'.

This depicted robust individuals partaking in the healthy pursuit of a pint or two of good beer in stark contrast to the, 'Mother's ruin' images of 'Gin Lane'.

# What's GIN A NAME?

Gin was nefariously known in earlier times by names intended to conceal its identity from the various officers and excise men determined to clamp down on the illegal elements of the trade.

'Ladies delight', 'Sleeper', 'Bob', 'Dilly Dally', 'Swallop' (from whore's wallop), 'Parliament', 'Cuckolds Delight' and 'Old Nig' (back slang) could all procure a glass of 'Mother's Ruin' from the lower establishments.

# GINNUENDO

The parliamentarian and reformer of the 17th century, John Wooton, described gin as an emolument of the lower classes.

'The poor have but two pleasures, sexual intercourse and drinking. Drinking is more popular on account of it being cheaper and with it's effects longer lasting'

# WHAT'S *In* GIN?

Gin derives its primary flavour from Juniper Berries. In fact, legally, gin can't be gin without Juniper Berries.

The nuances, flavours and aromas of different gin brands comes from the subtle additions of fruits and spices (known as 'botanicals') in an (often secret) carefully balanced mix to create the unique gin of a particular distillery.

The 'big four' botanicals, as they are known, are: Juniper, Coriander, Orris root and Angelica. Lemons, oranges, raspberries and other fruits all can play their part.

# KEEP
# GIN *Good*
# HEALTH

Gin was originally a herbal medicine, the juniper berries acting with the spirit to produce a powerful healing potion, as was supposed at the time.

It was purported to be good for diabetes, asthma and sciatica. It was also considered to work as a female contraceptive and a cure for male impotence (though presumably limited quantities should have been advised to avoid the opposite effect).

# GINVENTION

Gin and Tonic was invented in India. Tonic was introduced to gin or, more correctly, gin was introduced to tonic to make the medicine more palatable.

When the British occupied India (1858-1947) many officers and their families contracted Malaria, an infectious disease caught by contact with 'parasite carrying' mosquitos.

An infusion made from the bark of the Chinchona tree, where 'quinine' is derived, was used to ameliorate the symptoms and in some circumstances cure the Malaria. It was also considered preventative for the disease.

However the 'quinine' was very bitter and

impossible to drink in quantity so gin and lemon were added. Tonic waters contain little or no quinine today but one brand in particular, 'Fever Tree' maintains the connection with the past, if in name only.

# ORI-GIN

The Dutch made the original stuff and this was called Genever but it was maltier and more substantial than the clear spirit of London Dry Gin.

It was, however, and still is, very popular in Holland. In the Dutch war of Independence in the 1580's the British noted that the Dutch army fought with such fury after drinking quantities of 'Gen' that they nicknamed the stuff, 'Dutch Courage'.

The British, wanting much of the same kind of 'fighting spirit' in their troops, distilled the 'Gen' to a pure spirit before adding the juniper berries thus producing a more refined drink, mainly distilled in London.

# GINDESCRIBABLE

## *Tasting*

# EXPERIENCES

## Martin Millers Westbourne Gin

A favourite for the perfect gin and tonic. It has a higher alcohol content with a unique floral bouquet. Leaves you dangerously wanting more.

## Square Mile Gin

A good all rounder. It has wonderful notes of liquorice and citrus with a slightly spicy aftertaste. Good to put your money on.

## Colonel Fox's London Dry Gin

Probably has the most collectable bottle with it's brilliantly vivid 'Colonel Fox' illustration on the label. And the gin is also brilliant. It displays a slightly citron, hint of spice with a full flavour.

## D 1 London Gin

Makes a great gin and tonic and delicious gin cocktails. This is a very smooth gin with notes of citrus, liquorice and with the rare tinge of nettle.

## Portobello Road Gin

This is an exotic gin with complexity. It contains balanced and variable botanicals, exuberant in it's audacity, with herby finishing notes.

## Greenalls London Dry Gin

An interesting nasal experience of lemon, coriander and various secret botanicals. Crisp and fresh to the palate.

## 6 O'Clock Gin

A good time to start for this quaffing gin. A very smooth taste and its neutral nature gives it versatility as a cocktail component.

## Boodle's Gin

It has oodles of flavour and is full on the palate. It is generally floral in character with spicy subtleties.

## Sacred Gin

This is indeed the holy grail of the gin world. It exhibits a smooth flavour full of complicated botanicals with no sharp aftertaste.
Nectar of the god's.

## Fords Gin

A simple favourite. Citrus, fruits and spicy scents whirl around to create a heady mix of purity.

## Gilpins Gin

Made for martinis this superb distillation is extra dry with a simple melange of ingredients. Will hold your imagination as you rhapsodise over its minimalism.

## Tanqueray 10

A smooth gin of excellent distilling pedigree able to prove it's authority at the more competitive level. It's light, fragrant with touches of fruity crispness.

## Sipsmith's Gin

A natural favourite for it's zesty, unpretentious delivery of an exquisite 'riche en gout' gin, a veritable 'esprit formidable'. Smooth and refreshing.

## Botanist (Islay) Dry Gin

A strong willed gin with distinct flavour. Its herbaceous botanicals evoke a harsh depth of taste of the Hebrides that is not at all unpleasant.

# Dorothy Parker Gin (New York Distilling Company)

Named after Dorothy Parker, the New York wit and poet who had a life-long affection for gin martinis, inspiring her to write odes such as: "I like to have a martini, two at the very most, after three I'm under the table, after four I'm under the host".

# Old Curiosity Distillery Gin

A delicious gin made from floral botanicals from the Scottish Secret Herb Garden near Edinburgh, Scotland. Gincredibly, the ingredients have magical colour changing properties.

For example, the popular Chamomile and Cornflower flavoured gin changes from blue to pale pink when you add your tonic water.

# GINNNERS
## Medal Winners
## From *Around*
## *The* World

## Il Mio Gin,
## Denmark

A remarkable, fruity, delicate gin with a rapturous rhapsody of heady tones to tantalise the senses. The nose is complex, integrating lemon marmalade, lemon sorbet, lime, grapefruit and citrus grass alongside cinnamon, clove and juniper to complete the luxuriant repertoire.

On the palate the additional sensations

of raspberry, violet and grenadine excite the taste buds whilst the finish absorbs, in length, the nuances of bergamot, liquorice and Earl Grey tea. A lively gin with a generosity of spirit.

## Monopolowa Dry Gin, Austria

A robust gin that luxuriates on the palate, caressing the senses with fruits and subtle spices. It has a finish that emphasises the sweet, dry, floral nature of this most appetizing gin. A gin that celebrates and elevates itself with its own exuberance.

## The Source Cardrona, New Zealand

A bright, joyful gin, both subtle and nectareous, it has an abundance of melodic sensations of fruits and intriguing botanicals. Myrtle and jasmine float and combine upon the palate with delicate shades of rosemary and anise culminating in a smooth, beautiful, exquisite finish. A gin best savoured in quiet contemplation in aesthetic surroundings.

## Steinhart Gin,
## Nova Scotia, Canada

A clear, pure, entrancing gin with a lovely bouquet and harmonious notes of honeysuckle, rosewater, jasmine, lavender and pine.

Its strong, smooth countenance is ambrosial as it plays on the palate like a well-tuned Stradivarius.

It speaks of freshness and outdoors, of cool springs and fertile pastures. Quite simply, a very fine gin.

## Mcelroys Corruption,
## USA

A bold, unforgiving rumbustious offering that has got to be tried, tamed and tested. This is a gin, and you will know about it as soon as this strong but surprisingly smooth distillation is tasted. It carries the phalanx of botanicals and fruits of, arguably, it's more sophisticated cousins but it delivers with a refreshing directness.

A gin to drink with friends and laughter. Lots to like.


## Battle Standard 142 American Dry Navy Strength Gin, Virginia, USA

This 'bad boy' is 57% proof and packs a punch as strong as a broadside hitting a British Man O' War.

In spite of the 142's fire power it still contains all the gratifying essentials and complexity of a finely balanced gin.

Along with its aromatic fruits swims the bouillon of coriander, spice, white pepper and clove scents to give a hearty, heart-warming, lasting taste on the palate.

A boisterous gathering would be well served with this adventurous stalwart.

# Goodman's, Netherlands

A very nice, well rounded gin with an initially unspectacular nose that develops abundantly to tantalise the palate with its fragrant subtleness, its delicate floral notation and its quietude.

Lemon verbena, vanilla and sandalwood can be discerned with patient contemplation alongside a variety of herbaceous, nuanced essences of cardamom, wet pink peppercorns and basil. It's a nice quaffing gin that leaves one baffled and curious as to its origin and type.

A good all round gin for cocktails and G&T's.

# Dancing Dog, Oregon, USA

All is not what it seems with this genial gin. Its unpretentiousness combined with its amicability denies the frivolity of its name. A finely distilled gin from the Fox Den Distillery in Oregon, it performs immaculately when used in a martini, a gin cocktail or a classic gin and tonic. No simpleton, it has a full range of harmonious botanicals to delight and amuse the palate. Its wine equivalent would be a Chablis, or a light Burgundy.

## Principe De Los Apostoles, Argentina

From a region normally associated with good wine, this blissful, enticing spirit unfolds upon the palate with an unexpected sensory fulmination. The fruits and herbaceous botanicals release aromas of lemon, chocolate, rose, lavender and Earl Grey tea. It contains in one gulp the colourful characteristics of a sunny carnival, evoking the spirit of dance and innuendo.

## Durham Cask Aged Gin, UK

The naivety of youth (2014) in no way impairs the voluptuousness of this pleasing, award winning newcomer. The limited editions are rested in American bourbon and Spanish Oloroso casks, an aging process that give this gin its unique flavour and subtlety.

Tranquillity descends as the fragrant notes of bitter citrus, smooth oak, honeyed spice and juniper permeate the delicate reaches of the palate bringing a blissful, elysian tasting experience. Armchairs, fireplaces and soggy dogs are a perfect backdrop to the Durham experience.

# BE-GIN *In The* KITCHEN

Gin was taken at the table as a good accompaniment to meat dishes. Tasty dishes of quail, pheasant, veal, rabbit, hedgehog, boar, swan and venison were all the better for being eaten with a good sloshing of gin.

Gin was much cheaper than wine. Wine generally came from France, and was the subject of regular import bans as the wars raged between the French and the British.

Gin was considered to be much better for the digestion than the weaker beverages of Burgundy.

# GINPROVISE

You can make your own gin though using a still is a more extreme way of creating a few bottles because of the time, space and cost required.

Essentially, gin is made from pure distilled grain alcohol. A bottle of vodka provides the perfect base ingredient. To this you add juniper berries, spices and fruit peel to your own discerning choice.

Leave this for a month and sieve out the solids and it's a very personal, special bottle of gin.

# GINCLUDE

Botanicals of choice include juniper berries (obligatory), slice of ginger, hibiscus syrup, earl grey tea, cucumber, mint, rosemary, sage, basil, coriander, bergamot, angelica root and seeds, orris root, liquorice root, cinnamon, almond, cubeb, lime peel, grapefruit peel, saffron, frankincense and nutmeg,

Best not to put them all in at the same time though!

# GINDUSTRY

All gin is made from Neutral Spirits. These can be produced from grain, corn, grapes, sugar beets, sugarcane, tuber, or other fermented plant material.

In particular, large quantities of neutral alcohol are distilled from wine. Such a product made from grain is 'grain neutral spirit', while such a spirit made from grapes is called 'grape neutral spirit', or 'vinous alcohol'.

Neutral spirits can then be turned into vodka and gin by the addition of various ingredients generally known as botanicals. The flavour of juniper berries is a required ingredient of Gin.

How the botanicals are added to make the gin, whether by distillation or infusion, determines the different types of gin.

Although there are many brands of gin there are basically only 4 styles of manufacture; London Dry Gin, Bathtub Gin, 'Genever' and Old Tom.

## London Dry Gin

The requirements of making gin to the London Dry Gin standard are first and foremost, good quality alcohol for the base ingredient. This is low in methanol and with no added sugar.

Only water may be added to reduce the alcohol level. It is flavoured predominantly with juniper berries but other botanicals may be added, (see earlier list) and still keep the 'London Dry Gin' label.

# Bathtub Gin

Bathtub gin is a definition of gin that refers to a more amateur method of making gin.

It is where the fruit and spices are added to the base alcohol by infusion or compounding, i.e. not using botanical distillation as in the case of London Dry Gin.

The name derives from the 1920's prohibition era in the USA where illegal booze was made using temporary, household equipment to evade the law, often using low grade, sometimes poisonous ingredients.

The 'Bathtub' method is quite an acceptable method of gin making and some well known brands use this style. Connoisseurs, however, consider the taste to be inferior.

## Genever (Jenever)

This is the original Dutch style of gin making using a fine distilled malt wine.

Juniper berries and spices are added at the distillation stage and sugar is added.

Genever has a more robust flavour, distinctly different from gin made using a pure, clear spirit but its many advocates prefer no other.

## Old Tom

Old Tom is sweeter than London Dry Gin but less sweet than Genever. It's a sort of in-between stage in the development of gin.

The juniper berries are added afterwards as opposed to the distilling of the botanicals in a 'London Dry Gin'.

Triple distilled wheat spirit is used in some of the best brands with the botanicals infused in the last distillation.

# GINCREDULOUS

Amazingly, Old Tom Gin was dispensed from what must have been one of the earliest forms of vending machine ever to be introduced in England (between 1680 and 1750), where hence the name 'Old Tom' is derived.

So as not to disturb the real drunks inside the pub, certain establishments had a 'hole in the wall' outside. On the insertion of a coin it would dispense a shot of gin into your beaker, glass or other container on to, effectively, the street.

There was nothing mechanical about this process. On hearing the 'ching' of a penny a bar tender would send a shot of gin down the tube. This 'hole in the wall' was identified by a flat wooden plate above it in the shape of a cat, affectionately known as 'Old Tom'.

Apparently it was popular with young pickpockets and apprentices who did not have to present themselves to the landlord to enjoy their tot of 'Bob'.

# GIN TASTING

Gin snobs should only compare gin varieties by tasting them at room temperature with only a little water added.

This allows the positive and negative qualities of the gin to be highlighted. It is suggested that 5 gins should be tasted in one session.

A lesser quantity does not give a wide enough palette differentiation and more than 5 can reduce discernment due to the effects of alcohol altering the objectivity of the exercise.

It is best to avoid contentious foods (spicy, vinegary or sweet foods) a good hour before tasting.

Tobacco will also alter the effects of your tasting experience so a similar sanction should be applied. Several sessions of 5 are required to gain experience from the tastings and detailed notes should be made for each gin.

As with wine and whisky tasting, observations should include the colour, the clarity, the 'nose', the first taste impression (sweet, fruity, acidy, strong, heady, smooth, heavy, botanically flavoursome, pungent, biting, etc.) the aftertaste, the length (how long the taste stays on the palette) and the overall enjoyment.

A connoisseur is able to discern, differentiate and opine upon at least 50 different gins.

Once a selection of favourite gins is established these then should be tasted with the various quality tonics on the market or other mixers of choice. Further experimentation should include cocktails.

# WHAT SIN
## *The*
# GIN?

———— ⋈⋈⋈ ————

Some say you can drink a good gin neat, as you would a cognac, or just with ice, but this is not the norm. By far the most popular way of consuming a quality gin is adding a mixer, the most popular being tonic water, a combination that started in the days of the old British Raj in India.

The bitterness of the tonic creates a 'non sweet' flavour that is appreciated by those who also enjoy the occasional beer and would not thank you for a 'sweet' 'vodka and orange' or a 'rum and black'. The bottle of tonic also allows for pouring a stronger or weaker drink depending on taste.

Just about any fruit can also be used as a mixer, most popular being lime, lemon, raspberry, cranberry and orange.

# Not JUST Any TONIC

Most tonic waters now contain little or no quinine although their original purpose was to deliver this precious health-giving component to alleviate the symptoms of Malaria fever.

The USA Food & Drug Administration (FDA) limits quinine content in tonic water to 83 milligrams per litre. The daily dose for the therapeutic prevention of malaria is 500-1000 mgs. Therefore you would have to consume 10 litres of tonic or 50 G&T's per day to stave off the disease!

There are many tonic waters now available and preferences are just as subjective to the drinker's taste as the myriad of gins on the market.

The default mix is to add twice the amount of tonic water to the gin but just a splash from the bottle may do the trick. Obviously this is down to individual taste. Some dispense with tonic altogether and drink it neat.

The Gin Snob will always have an opinion on which tonic water goes best with which gin and this can go to the extremes of 'gin snobs' refusing a G&T if their perfect combination is not on offer.

Most good tonic waters make a perfect accompaniment to most good gins and getting the perfect balance of a G&T to suit your palate is really the most important thing.

Interestingly, quinine is a fluorescent substance and a G&T that 'glows' in bright sunlight contains a higher content of quinine.

The largest producer of tonic water is Coca Cola with their 'Schweppes' brand and they have invested heavily on up-marketing their products to try to win back a greater share of the market, lost to the new kids on the block who have taken advantage of the upsurge, such as 'Fever Tree' and 'Fentimans', amongst other newcomers.

Here is a selection of some of the current most popular tonics available, for those wishing to compliment a good gin with a quality tonic.

Tastes can vary noticeably or imperceptibly and are very subjective to the individual, the vocabulary to describe these tastes being limited to words like zesty, refreshing, sweet, bitter, effervescent and fruity.

Experimentation is the key to pairing your favourite gin to a compatible tonic in order to achieve the perfect G&T, created for your individual taste.

## Fever Tree

Fever Tree, the company who's name reflects the origin of tonic water; a tree bark infusion to treat malaria fever, have taken the humble tonic to a higher level, identifying with the revival of gin drinking in the UK and elsewhere.

They have several varieties. Indian, Naturally Light and Elderflower are particular favourites with gin connoisseurs.

Gin Twin:
SIPSMITH GIN

## Boylan Heritage

This tonic with 'added citrus' makes a very pleasant mixer. Great for 'on the go' imbibing as it does not need the addition of a slice of lime or lemon for a zesty taste.

Gin Twin:
BOMBAY SAPPHIRE

## Merchant's Heart

This company turns tonic water and other spirit enhancers into an art form. Made with 'Bikan Yuso', as the story goes, 'a sense of beauty and playful imagination'. But there's nothing 'ippan' (ordinary) about the taste of their classic tonic that pairs well with most good gins.

Gin Twin:
FORD'S LONDON DRY

## Schweppes Original

This is still the most popular tonic. It is a well-produced, basic all round crowd pleaser. Although not as 'on trend' as its newer contemporaries, it still serves as a good pleasant mixer. The Schweppes 'slimline' tonic also continues to be a best seller... with fewer calories!

Gin Twin:
GORDON'S LONDON DRY GIN

## Schweppes Indian

This is a cut above the regular Schweppes and delivers a tonic with attitude, a robust flavour with a full bouquet of flavours.

Gin Twin:
BEEFEATER 24

## Bradley's Bourbon Barrel

Aged in oak bourbon barrels before bottling, it's the 'grand cru classic' of tonics. A perfect combination for 'meaty' gins with a good juniper kick.

Gin Twin:
BLOOM LONDON DRY


## Fentiman's

This is a bold and loud tonic that simply does not want to be just the accompaniment to the main 'gin' program. It is a complex drink with a full range of fruity and herbaceous botanicals all of it's own and will compliment the finest gins.

Gin Twin:
MILLER'S DRY GIN

## Bramley and Gage

Bramley and Gage's 'distillers' tonic is, according to them, the distiller's tonic of choice because of it's ability to create a perfect G&T from all gins. It is truly a quality product of excellent depth to mix with gins of good quality.

Gin Twin:
BLACKWOOD'S


## Bottle Green

'Classic', 'Light', 'Elderflower' and 'Pink' are some of the choices from this successful company and are available in quality bars and specialty gin lounges, a combination of style and good taste.

Gin Twin:
THE BOTANIST

## Jack Rudy Cocktail Company

The 'Jack Rudy Cocktail Company' specialize in old style mixer drinks to make classic cocktails and they've been doing it for a long time - almost 80 years.

Their 'classic tonic syrup' and 'elderflower tonic' just can't be beaten.

Gin Twin:
BURLEIGH'S EXPORT
STRENGTH

# GINDULGENCE

Gin is indisputably the most creatively used spirit for making cocktails, the most famous being the Dry Martini.

Although the vodka version was stylized in the Bond movies, a true Dry Martini is made from gin (5 parts), dry vermouth (1 part) poured over semi-crushed ice, with a green olive floating on top. Always use a gin of personally assured quality when mixing gin cocktails.

Gin and It is also a well known cocktail and this is made in much the same way as a Dry Martini but using sweet vermouth and garnishing with a cherry instead of an olive to create a sweeter cocktail ('It' is short for 'Italian Vermouth').

There are several hundred 'gin cocktails', the recipes of which could fill several books. Some favourites are:

# Tom Collins
(Find a big glass)

The ratios:
2 Gin, ½ fresh lemon, ½ simple syrup
Add lots of ice, 2 lemon wedges and any fresh fruit you can lay your hands on (raspberries, strawberries and kiwis are always good) and slices of cucumber.
You should add soda water to serve.

Gin Twin: PLYMOUTH

# Singapore Sling
(It's a belter!)

The ratios:
1½ Gin, ½ cherry brandy, ¼ triple sec, ¼ Benedictine liqueur, 4 pineapple juice, ½ lime juice, ½ grenadine syrup, 2 ice, slice pineapple, 1 maraschino cherry.

Gin Twin: BEEFEATER LONDON GARDEN

# Gimlet
(A drink to stave off 'rickets')

The ratios:
1½ Gin, 1 lime juice, ¼ simple syrup, ice, lime.

Gin Twin: CAORUNN GIN

# Pink Lady
(Packs a punch and not just for ladies)

The ratios:
½ Gin, ½ applejack, ¾ lemon juice, ¼ grenadine, 1 egg white, ice.

Gin Twin: ROCK ROSE GIN

# Vesper
(A rather large, bond-like martini)

The ratios:
3 Gin, 1 Vodka, ½ Lillet Blanc

Gin Twin: BOMBAY DRY GIN

# Negroni
## ('Cocktailing' made simple)

It's the original 1:1:1 cocktail (equal parts gin, vermouth, and Campari). Tweak the components to taste, most people like a little more gin.

Gin Twin: HENDRICK'S GIN

# French 75
## (Best 'tale of two cities', London and Paris)

The ratios:
1 Gin, 1 champagne, ½ fresh lemon, ½ simple syrup add zest peel of choice to serve.

Gin Twin: HEPPLE GIN

# The Bee's Knee's
## (And it really is!)

The ratios:
2 Gin, 1 lime juice,  ½ lemon juice,
¾  honey syrup, ice, lime.

Gin Twin: WHITTAKERS


# Gin Rickey
## (Originated in Washington D.C.)

The ratios:
1 ½ Gin, 1 lime juice, ¼ sugar, ice,
lime, seltzer water.

Gin Twin: DOROTHY PARKER

# Aviation
## (It's a flyer!)

This cocktail utilizes Maraschino liqueur. Aviation (sometime known as aviation fuel!)

The ratios:
3 Gin, 1 Maraschino liqueur, 1 lemon juice. Serve with a Maraschino cherry.

Gin Twin: AVIATION AMERICAN GIN

# GINBIBING

Gin Touring is a great way to travel.
Although many countries already have, or are developing a gin culture, gin's natural home is the United Kingdom of Great Britain and Northern Ireland.
The gin delights the regions of the UK are second to none.

## London

As you might expect, London boasts a multitude of gin distilleries and gin 'palaces'.
The difficult job of choosing products from the popular distilleries in London was a challenge for our team but with so many available it is impossible to list them all.

Gins produced in London:

Half Hitch Gin, Camden; Fifty Eight Gin, Hackney Downs; Bimber Gins, North Acton; SW4 London Dry Gin, Clapham; City of London Dry Gin, The city; Sipsmith Distilleries, Chiswick; Becketts Gin, Kingston upon Thames; Butlers Gin, Hackney Wick; Portobello Road Gin Co., Notting Hill; Victory Cold Gin, Bermondsey; Dodds Gin, Battersea; East London Liquor Company, Mile End; Little Bird Gin, Peckham; Sacred Pink Grapefruit Gin, Highgate; Lensens Old Tom, Bermondsey.

Of the literally thousands of bars, pubs, lounges, clubs and hostelries in London where it's possible to enjoy a classic gin and tonic, or a gin cocktail, these are some of the favourites though not necessarily the best.

Where to taste:
City of London Distillery, Smithfield; Coburg Bar, Mayfair; East London Liquor

Company, Mile End; Four Thieves, Clapham Junction; The Gibson, Old Street; Gin Tonica, Westbourne; Holborn Dining Room, Holborn; The London Gin Club, Soho; Mr. Foggs Gin Parlour, Covent Garden; Worship Street Whistling Club, Hackney Shoreditch;

# Scotland

Scotland produces more than 70% of the UK's gin. It is home to the major distilleries of Gordon's, Tanqueray and Hendrick's. A selection of products from some of the smaller distilleries, chosen by our tasting team, is listed here.

Gins produced in Scotland:
Kintyre Gin, Campbeltown; Wild Island Botanical Gin, Isle of Colonsay; Sea Glass Gin, Deerness, Orkney; Indian Summer Gin, Huntley, Aberdeenshire; Rock Rose Gin, Thurso, Caithness; Eden Mill Gin; St. Andrew's; El:Gin, Elgin; Isle of Harris Gin, Isle of Harris; Misty Isle Gin, Isle of Skye;

Loch Ness Gin, Dores, Inverness; Lussa Gin, Isle of Jura; Mikkelmas Gin, Orkney; Porters Gin, Aberdeen; Kirkjuvagr Orkney, Kirkwall, Orkney; Shetland Reel Gin, Shetland.

Our tasters concentrated their research only in Glasgow and Edinburgh and these gin joints were recommended for a visit.

Where to taste:
One Square, Edinburgh; Heads and Tales, Edinburgh; Mother's, Edinburgh; 56 North, Edinburgh; The Jolly Botanist, Edinburgh; Gin 71, Glasgow & Edinburgh; The Finnieston, Glasgow; The Alston Bar & Beef, Glasgow; Tabac, Glasgow.

# Wales

Though a smaller player in the Gin game than England and Scotland, Wales has some unique offerings of the silver nectar. They also produce one of the only certified organic gins in the UK.

Gins produced in Wales:
Da Mhile Gin, Llandysul; Brecon Gin, Brecon Beacons; Eccentric Old Tom, Llantrisant; Forager Gin, Snowdonia; DYFI, Corris.

Our tasters enjoyed a tipple at:
Bar 44, Cardiff; Gin at 6, Swansea; The Potted Pig, Cardiff; Lab 22, Cardiff; Hogarth's, Swansea.

# Northern Ireland

Northern Ireland has a long tradition of distilling and its gins are exceptional. Here are but a few of them.

Gins produced in Northern Ireland:
Jawbox Classic Gin, Belfast; Shortcross Gin, Downpatrick, Co. Down; Copeland Gin, Saintfield; Boatyard Gin, Co. Fermanagh; Belfast 1912, Portaferry, Co. Down.

Taster's choice was:
Echlinville House, Belfast; The Cuan,

Strongford; Muriel's Café Bar, Belfast; Harbour Gin Bar, Portrush; Granary Bar, Newry.

# Yorkshire

Some fine gins are to be had from the UK's largest county. We think the ones listed are very good but there are quite a few more not mentioned here to choose from.

Gins produced in Yorkshire
Mason's Gin, Bedale; Raisethorpe Gin, Malton; Slingsby Gin, Harrogate; Whittakers Gin, Nidderdale; Sir Robin of Locksley Gin, Sheffield.

And the indefatigable tasters found to their delights some excellent hostelries.

Where to taste
The Lazy Lounge, Leeds; Bora, Bora, York; The Gin Lounge, Ilkley; Great Gatsby, Sheffield.

# The West Country

The West Country lays claim to Britain's oldest gin distillery, The Plymouth Distillery, Cornwall, makers of Plymouth Gin.

Gins produced in the West Country:
as well as Plymouth Gin's rivals for excellence are:
Curio Gin, Lizard Peninsula; Wicked Wolf Gin, Exmoor; Dorset Dry Gin, Dorset; Tarquin's Gin, Wadebridge, Cornwall.

And just when we thought they couldn't take another drop, the tasters uncover more gems hiding in the West Country.

Where to taste:
The Milk Thistle, Bristol; Hotel du Vin, Poole; The Magdalen Chapter, Exeter; Hotel Tresanton, St. Mawes, Cornwall, The Swan, Wedmore, Somerset.

# GINFO

~ Strane Uncut London Dry Gin (made in Sweden) is reputed to be the world's strongest gin with an ABV (Alcohol By Volume) reading of a whopping 76%. A measure of this gin is the equivalent in alcohol to a whole bottle of wine.

~ Gin and Tonic was invented by the British in India.

~ Gin must have juniper berries to be legally called gin.

~ World Gin Day is the second Saturday in June.

~ Plague doctors used masks that contained juniper berries to ward off the sickness.

~ Juniper oil is a flea repellent.

~ Pink gin is made from gin, angostura bitters and water.

~ A gin Martini is better stirred than shaken.

~ Gin has 134 million entries on Google, and counting!

~ The flavours in London Dry Gin are distilled, not added afterwards to the gin.

~ A pure London Dry Gin cannot have any added water.

~ Plymouth Gin can only legally be thus called if it is distilled in Plymouth.

~ London Dry Gin can be made anywhere as the name refers to the style of gin making.

~ Nolet's Reserve Dry Gin, with a hefty ABV of 52.3% is one of the most expensive, commercially available gins on the market at about £500 per 75cl bottle.

~ Probably the world's most expensive bottle of gin is Surrey based, Silent Pool's hand painted, 9 litre bottle coming in at a mere £5000 per bottle.

~ Aldi's own label gin was voted as being one of the highest quality gins on the market (2017) at a bargain price of £9.65.

~ The UK is the world's largest exporter of gin.

~ The largest London gin distillery is Beefeater Gin.

~ Gin only got popular in the USA during the Prohibition era in the 1920's. It was the easiest spirit to make clandestinely.

~ A 'Tequini' is a gin Martini made using Tequila.

~ W.C. Fields reputedly drank about 2.5 litres of gin a day starting with a martini before breakfast and one immediately afterwards.

~ Gin started life as a medicine thought to cure, among other things: gout, palsy, swamp fever, pox, impotence, cowardice and drunkenness.

~ Genever, as the first gin was called, was given to Dutch soldiers in battle to give them 'Dutch Courage'.

~ Quinine, a constituent in tonic water, is fluorescent and glows vividly in ultra violet light and this effect can be observed in sunshine.

~ The 'Gimlet' (gin with lime juice) was created by the British navy to stop scurvy though was only popular with officers, the rum ration being the ratings tot of choice.

~ Gin was much cheaper than milk in 17th century Britain. It was said that mothers would feed small amounts to their babies which presumably made them sleep more.

~ People in the Philippines drink more gin than those in any other country.

~ In 1923, in the USA and England the 'Gin Twist' was all the rage (as they said back then), a combination of gin, lemon juice, simple syrup and hot water.

~ In England in the early 16th century a glass of gin without a piece of gingerbread was considered poor fayre indeed according to the chronicler of the day, Samuel Johnstone.

~ 1823 was the year of the 'Hot Gin Twist', a hot toddy to keep the colds and flu's away from the busy London workers. Best drunk early in the morning.

~ You can buy more than 1200 different gins on the internet.

~ Gin and tomato juice was the hangover cure of choice for New Yorkers in 1928, according to some Manhattan bar owners who would serve this cure for breakfast (after administering the problem the night before!).

~ Juniper used in gin is picked wild rather than cultivated.

~ Quinine, as used in tonic water, is good for 'leg cramps'.

~ Gin snobs should only compare gin varieties by tasting them at room temperature with only a little water added.

~ Gin snobs seek an exquisite and elusive gin. They are prepared to spend a good deal of their time and money in pursuit of nuances of perfection, imperceptible to anyone else.

A perfect martini should be made by filling a glass with gin then waving it in the general direction of Italy.

*Noel Coward*

I exercise strong self control. I never drink anything stronger than gin before breakfast.

*W.C. Fields*

And remember...
DRY GIN-UARY
is better than
DRY JANUARY!

Researched and written
by Jamien Bailey